MY FIRST SCIENCE TEXTBOOK

Protons
and
Neutrons

Written by Mary Wissinger
Illustrated by Harriet Kim Anh Rodis

Created and edited by John J. Coveyou

Science, Naturally!
An imprint of Platypus Media, LLC
Washington, D.C.

My First Science Textbook: Protons and Neutrons
Copyright © 2021, 2020, 2016 Genius Games, LLC
Originally published by Genius Games, LLC in 2016

Written by Mary Wissinger
Illustrated by Harriet Kim Anh Rodis with Uzuri Designs
Created and edited by John J. Coveyou

Published by Science, Naturally!
English hardback first edition • 2016 • ISBN: 978-1-945779-00-8
    Second edition • October 2020
English paperback first edition • September 2021 • ISBN: 978-1-938492-45-7
English eBook first edition • 2016 • ISBN: 978-1-945779-06-0
English board book first edition • 2016 • ISBN: 978-1-945779-03-9
Bilingual (En/Sp) paperback first edition • September 2021 • ISBN: 978-1-938492-46-4
Bilingual (En/Sp) eBook first edition • September 2021 • ISBN: 978-1-938492-47-1

Enjoy all the titles in the series:
    Atoms • Los átomos
    Protons and Neutrons • Los protones y los neutrones
    Electrons • Los electrones

Teacher's Guide available at the Educational Resources page of ScienceNaturally.com.

Published in the United States by:
    Science, Naturally!
        An imprint of Platypus Media, LLC
    725 8th Street, SE, Washington, D.C. 20003
    202-465-4798 • Fax: 202-558-2132
    Info@ScienceNaturally.com • ScienceNaturally.com

Distributed to the trade by:
    National Book Network (North America)
        301-459-3366 • Toll-free: 800-462-6420
        CustomerCare@NBNbooks.com • NBNbooks.com
    NBN international (worldwide)
        NBNi.Cservs@IngramContent.com • Distribution.NBNi.co.uk

Library of Congress Control Number: 2021936484

10 9 8 7 6 5 4 3 2 1

Printed in Canada

Expand and extend the content in this book with our extensive Teacher's Guide. Available for free download at ScienceNaturally.com.

I'm Pete the Proton!

I'm positively charged to meet you!
I'm a subatomic particle.
Our introduction is overdue!

When it comes to an element's identity, protons are the defining trait.

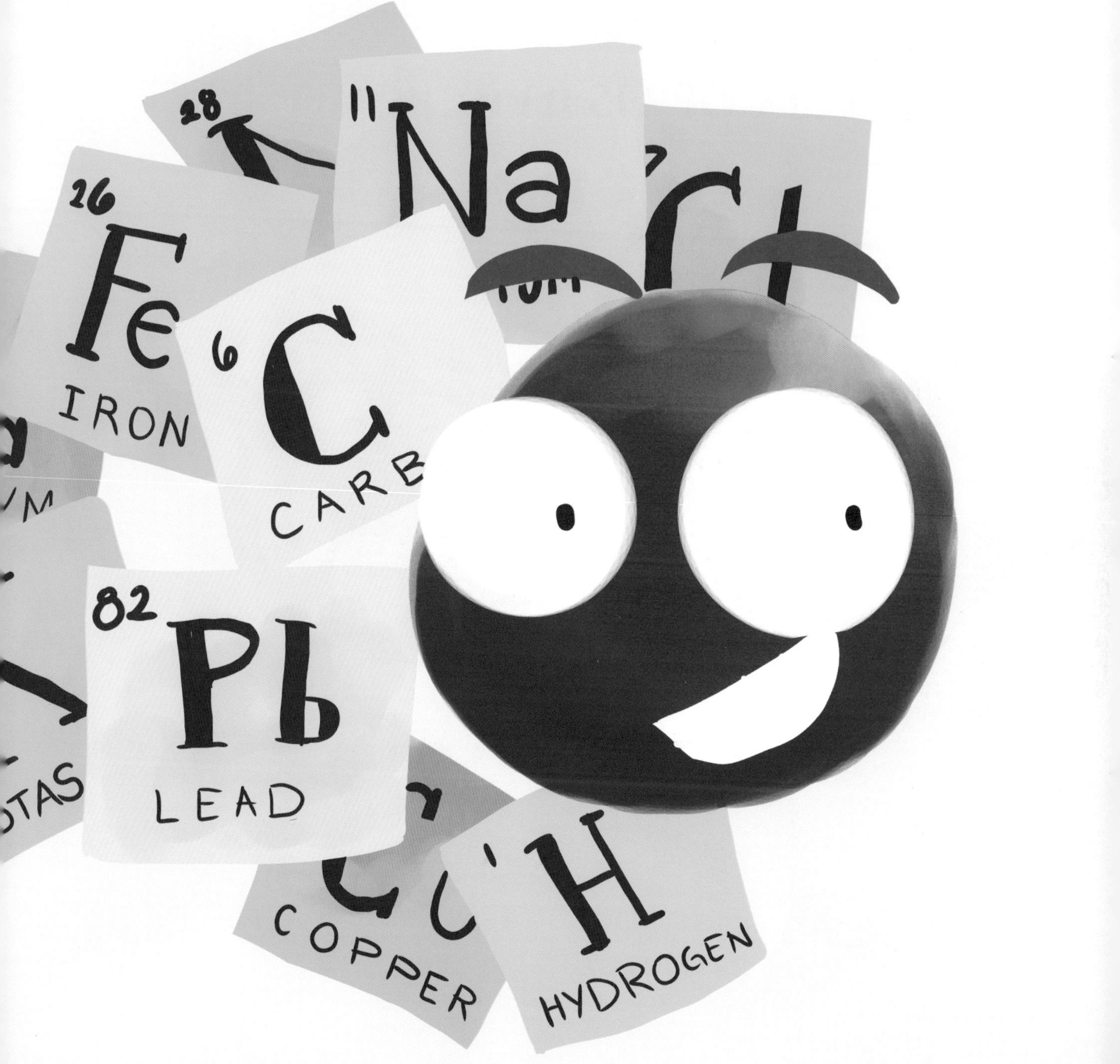
28
11
Na
26
Fe
IRON
6
C
CARB
82
Pb
LEAD
COPPER
H
HYDROGEN

Find six of us in carbon.

In oxygen, find eight.

11

This is Ned the Neutron.

He's neutral, and important, too.

He makes up
nearly half of
everything's mass.

So he makes up nearly half of you.

Protons and neutrons are tiny.
You can't see us with your eye.

But no matter the
state of matter,
guess what?

You'll find me and this guy.

Our playground is the nucleus and it's where we like to stay.

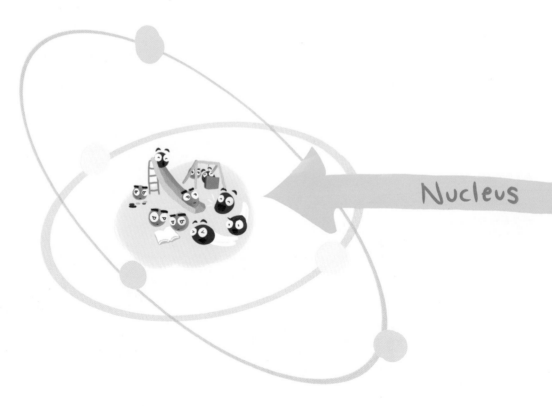

Nucleus

Isotopes have extra neutrons...

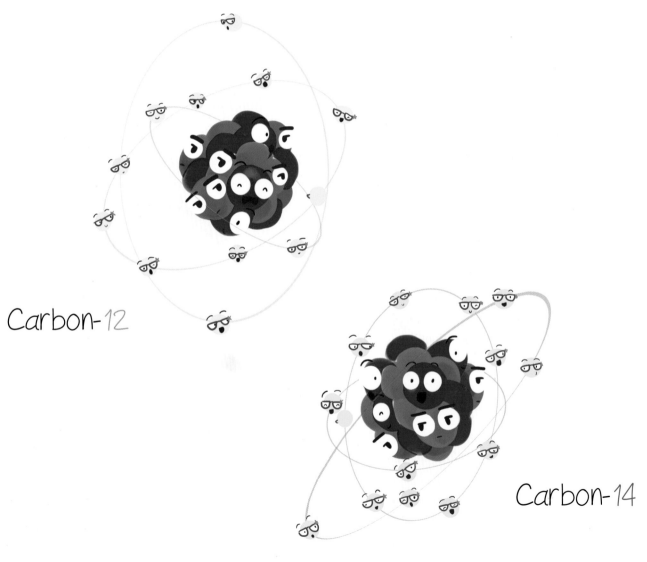

Carbon-12

Carbon-14

but too many neutrons
may decay.

The strong force keeps us stuck like glue.

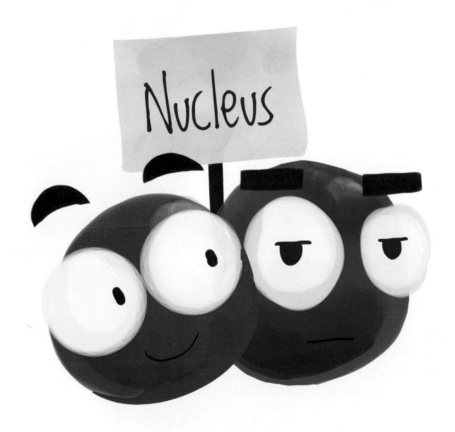

Splitting us is a tough mission.

Our reaction?
Explosively energetic!
It's called nuclear fission.

I'm attracted to electrons.
Our charges are equal
and opposite.

Ned is unaffected,
but my attraction is
quite passionate!

When protons, neutrons, and electrons team up,

⁵B
BORON

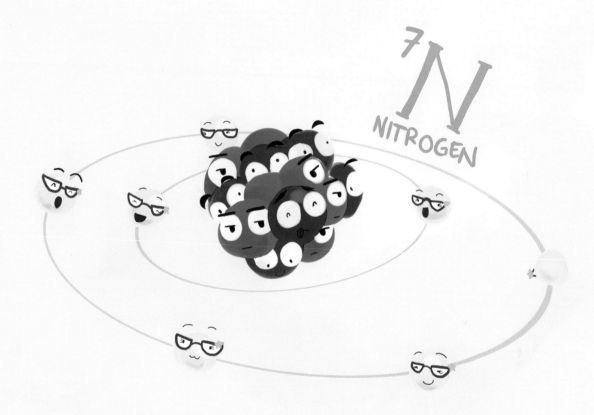

we are the best of friends.

Together, we build the universe.
Our influence never ends!

Glossary

ATOMS: The building blocks for all matter in our universe. They are so small that you can't see them, and are made up of even smaller particles called protons, neutrons, and electrons.

ATOMIC NUMBER: The number of protons in an atom determines an element's atomic number, which is used to categorize elements.

CHARGE: An electric charge is a property of matter. There are two types of electric charges: positive and negative. Protons have a positive charge and electrons have a negative charge.

DECAY: The breakdown of an atom's nucleus, which releases energy and matter through radiation.

ELECTRONS: Very teeny particles with a negative electric charge. Electrons travel around the nucleus of every atom.

ELEMENT: A pure substance made of one type of atom.

FORCE: The push or pull on something when it interacts with something else. A force can cause an object to move faster, slow down, stay in place, or change shape.

GAS: Air-like substances that have no set shape or volume because the molecules in them are spread very far apart and move very quickly. A gas can expand to fill a whole space.

ISOTOPES: Two or more atoms of the same element with the same number of protons but a different number of neutrons.

LIQUID: A substance that flows freely and has volume but no set shape, like water or oil. The molecules in liquids stay close together, but they can move freely.

MASS: A measure of how much matter is in an object. Mass is different from weight because the mass of an object never changes, but its weight will change based on its location in the universe.

MATTER: Anything in the universe that takes up space and has mass. Matter makes up everything around you.

MOLECULE: A group of atoms that are bonded together to form the smallest unit of a substance that has all the properties of that substance. For example, a water molecule is the smallest unit that is still water.

NEUTRAL: An object with no electric charge, or with equal numbers of positively charged protons and negatively charged electrons.

NEUTRONS: Very teeny particles with no electric charge, found in the nucleus of most atoms.

NUCLEAR FISSION: Splitting atoms apart into smaller pieces, which releases a lot of energy.

NUCLEUS: The center of an atom, made up of protons and neutrons.

PARTICLES: Tiny, singular bits of matter that can range in size from subatomic particles, such as electrons, to ones large enough to be seen, such as particles of dust floating in sunlight.

PROTONS: Very teeny particles with a positive electric charge. Protons are in the nucleus of every atom.

SOLID: A form of matter that has a set shape and volume because the molecules in it are packed close together and do not move much. The shape of a solid only changes when a force is applied.

STATE OF MATTER: The way matter acts, based on temperature or pressure. For example, ice (solid) melts into water (liquid), then evaporates into steam (gas).

SUBATOMIC PARTICLE: A particle that is smaller than an atom and exists within it, like protons, neutrons, or electrons.

TRAIT: Something that makes an object, person, or other living thing different from others.

UNIVERSE: All of time and space and their contents, including planets and stars, and all other forms of matter and energy.

Discover the
My First Science Textbook series

Book 2

Book 1

MY FIRST SCIENCE TEXTBOOK

Atoms

Written by Mary Wissinger
Illustrated by Harriet Kim Anh Rodis

MY FIRST SCIENCE TEXTBOOK

Protons
and
Neutrons

Written by Mary Wissinger
Illustrated by Harriet Kim Anh Rodis

Book 3

MY FIRST SCIENCE TEXTBOOK

Electrons

Written by Mary Wissinger
Illustrated by Harriet Kim Anh Rodis

Protons and Neutrons:
Hardback ISBN: 978-1-945779-00-8
Paperback ISBN: 978-1-938492-45-7
Bilingual (En/Sp) ISBN: 978-1-938492-46-4

Atoms:
Hardback ISBN: 978-1-945779-02-2
Paperback ISBN: 978-1-938492-41-9
Bilingual (En/Sp) ISBN: 978-1-938492-39-6

Electrons:
Hardback ISBN: 978-1-945779-01-5
Paperback ISBN: 978-1-938492-48-8
Bilingual (En/Sp) ISBN: 978-1-938492-49-5

8 x 8" • 32 pages • Ages 2-7
Hardback: $14.99 • Paperback: $12.95
Also available in eBook and board book!

Science, Naturally! | Sparking curiosity through reading

ScienceNaturally.com
Info@ScienceNaturally.com